Rainforest Animals and Jungle Animals Easy to Read :Large Print Dot-to-Dot Book Puzzles From 150 to 600 Dots

By Laura's Dot to Dot Therapy

How To Use This Book

Hi! We're so glad you're a lover of puzzles and dot connecting- we are too!

Connecting the dots in this book is simple- just relax and follow the numbers in consecutive order, drawing a straight line between each one. Dot 1 will connect to dot 2 and so on and so forth until there are no more dots to connect. There's always another dot and you'll always find it. Connect every dot to discover the beautiful images they create.

In case you get lost or can't find a dot, never stress- there's an answer key at the back of the book that will show you exactly where each dot connects to the next. If you want to color your images, we encourage you to do so! Feel free to try all different colors and coloring mediums for your images!

If you find any errors or omissions in this book, just email us at Laurasdottodot@gmail.com, let us know, and we will send you a free book to make up for it! We want you to have the best dot to dot experience!

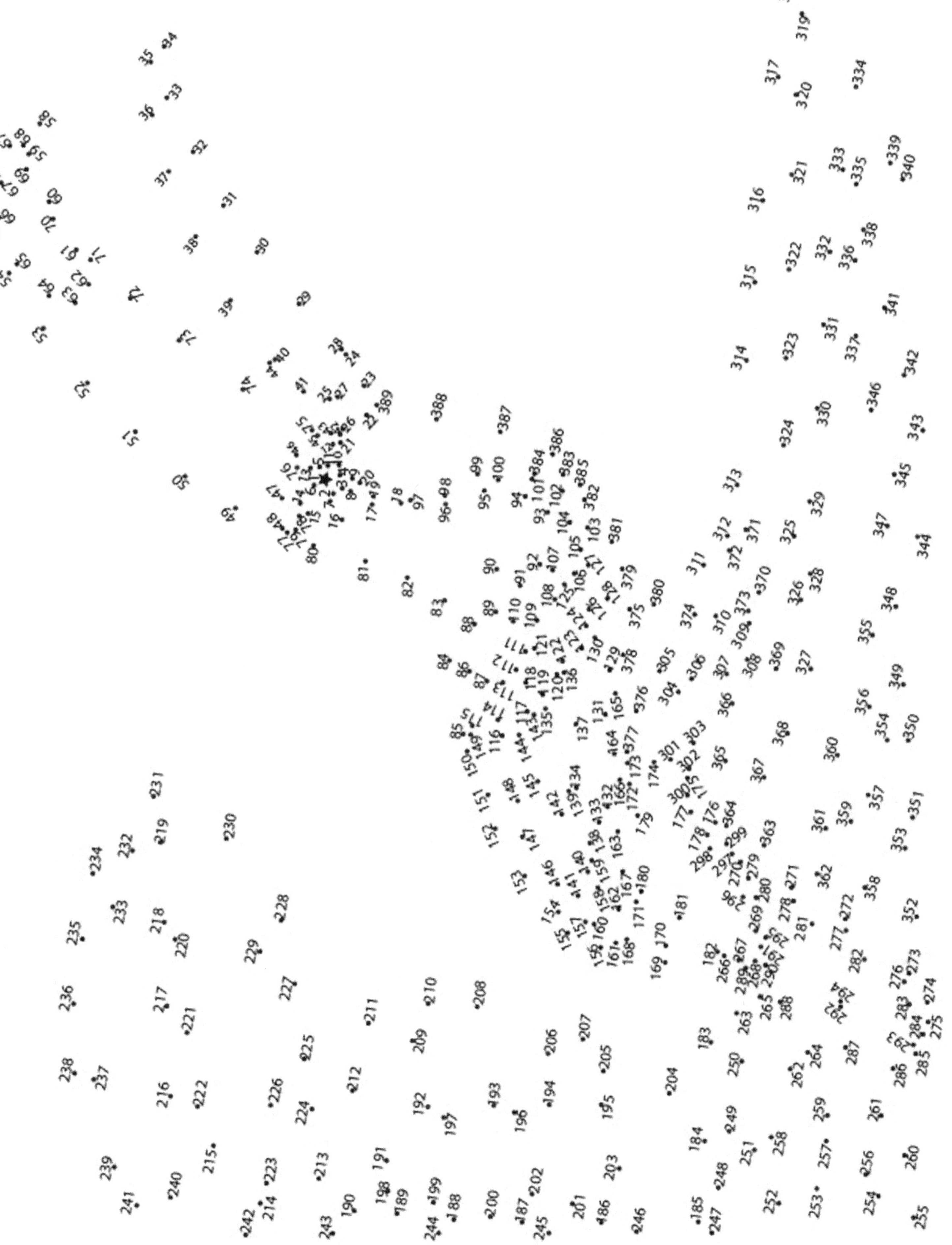

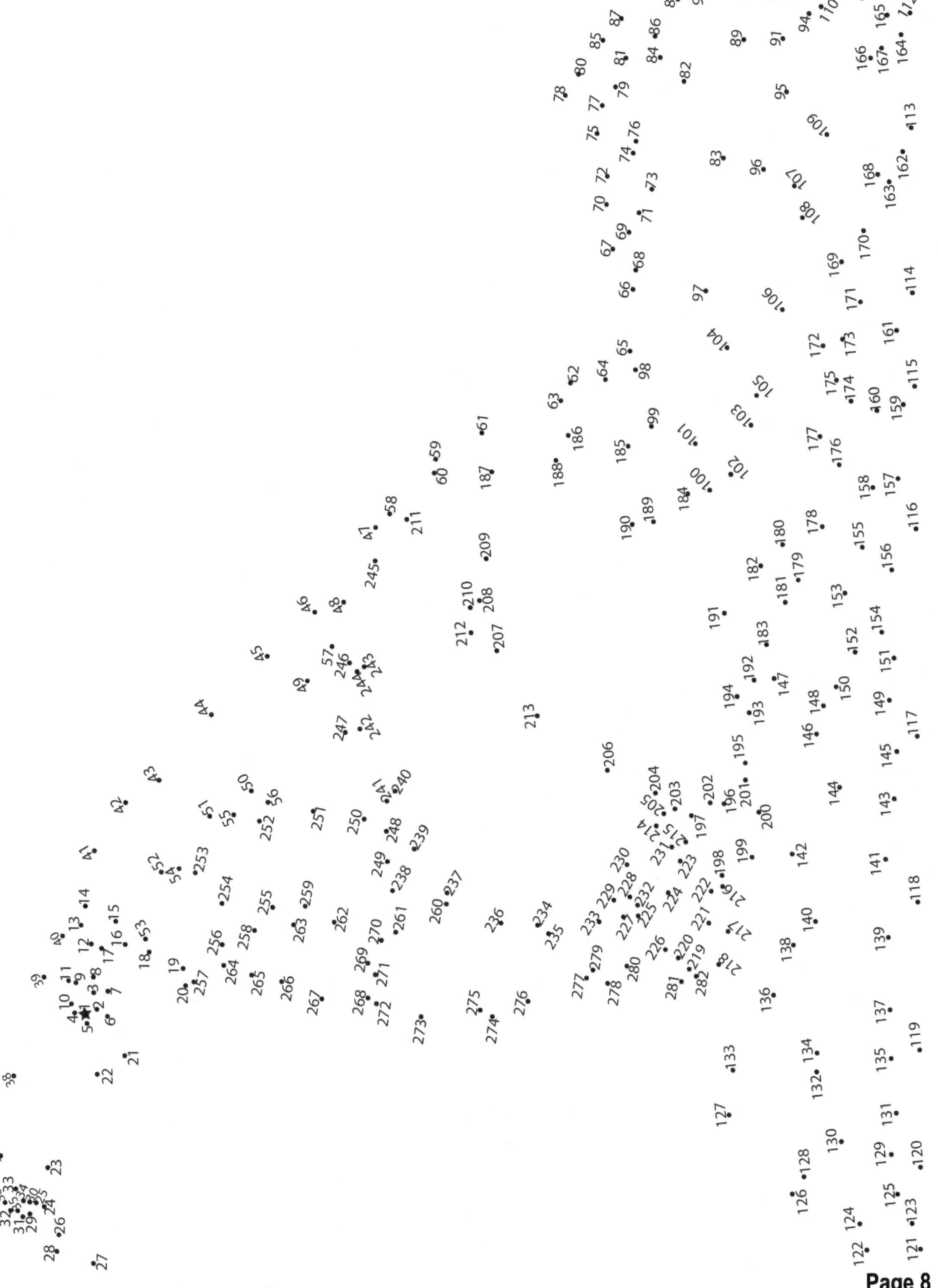

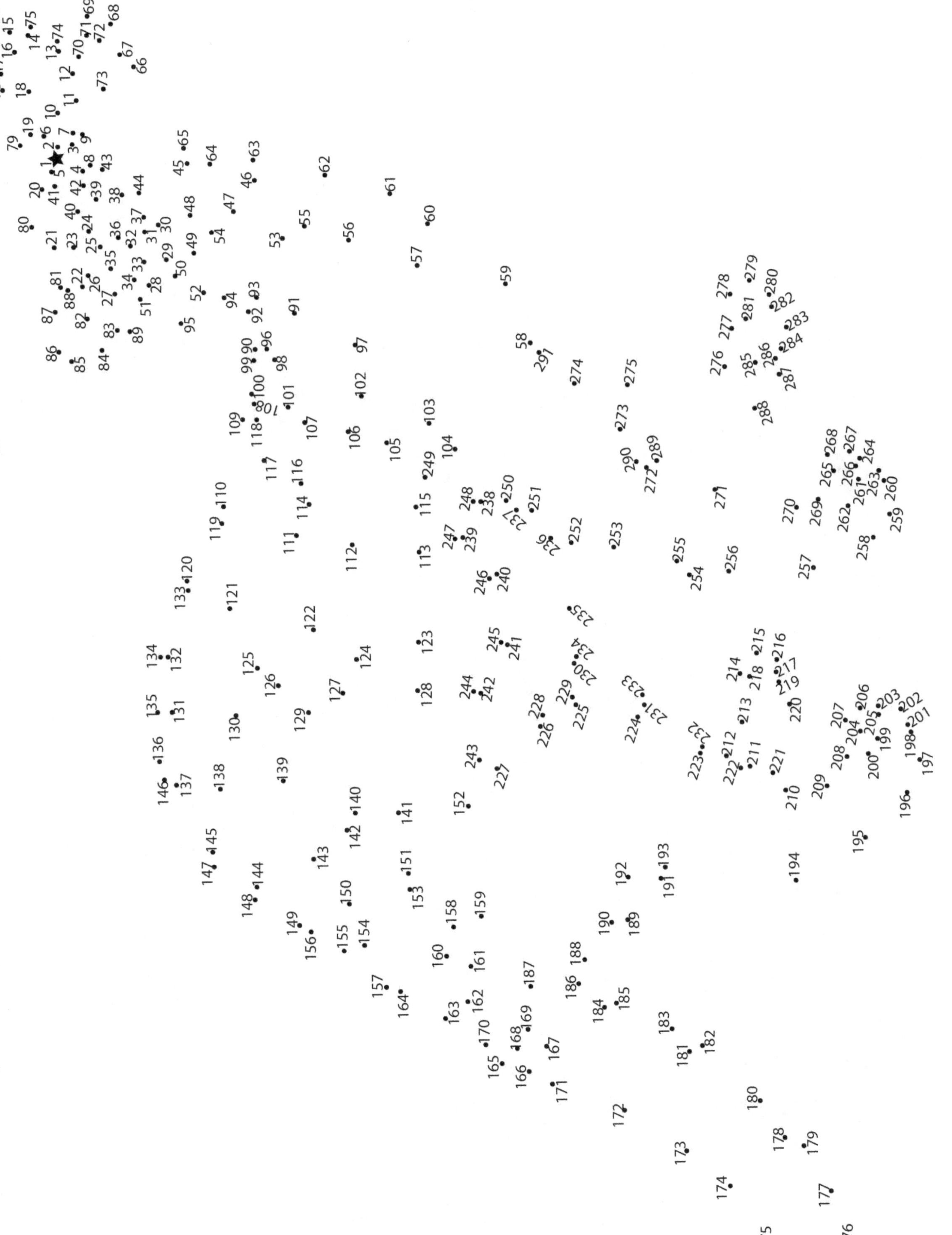

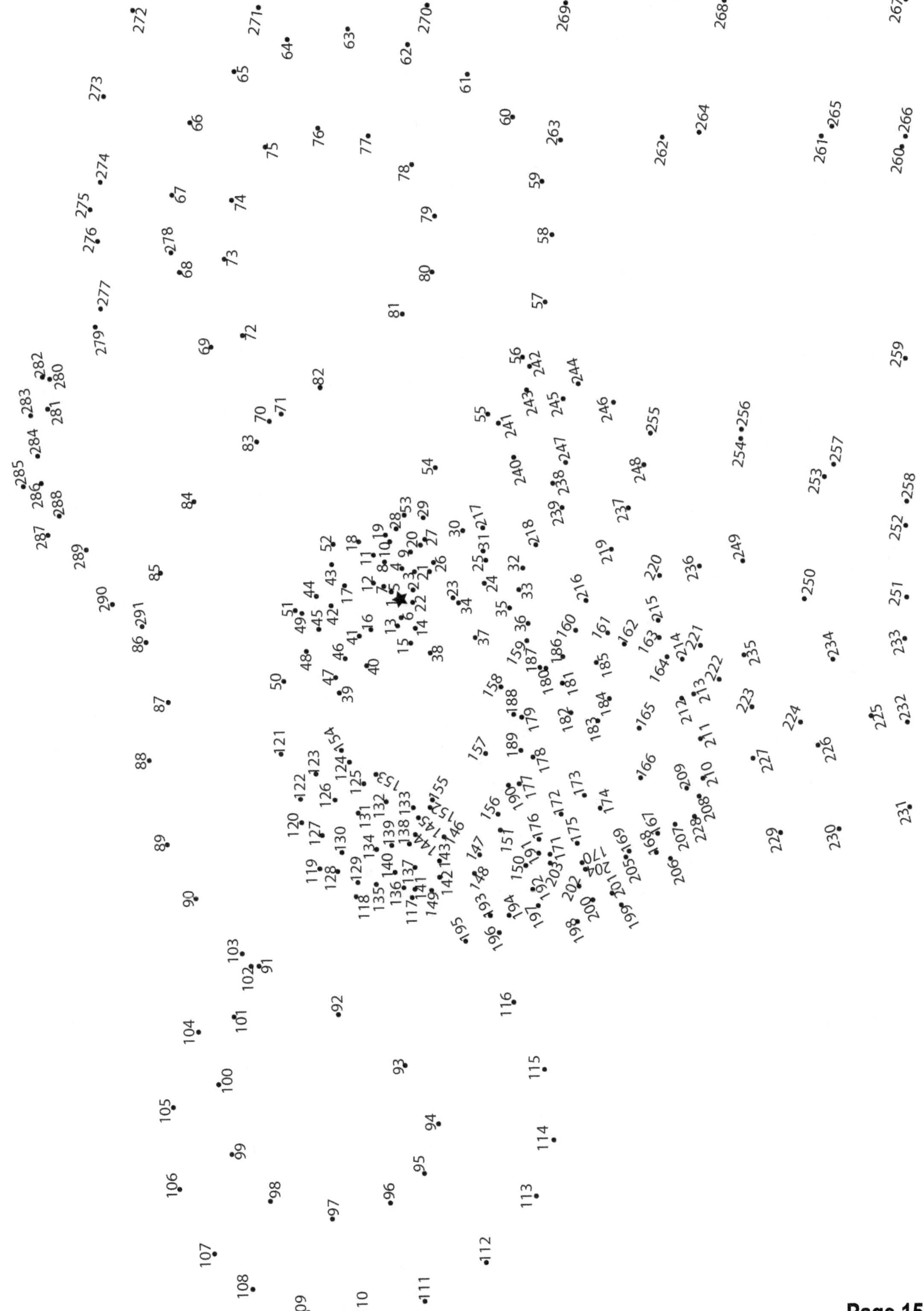

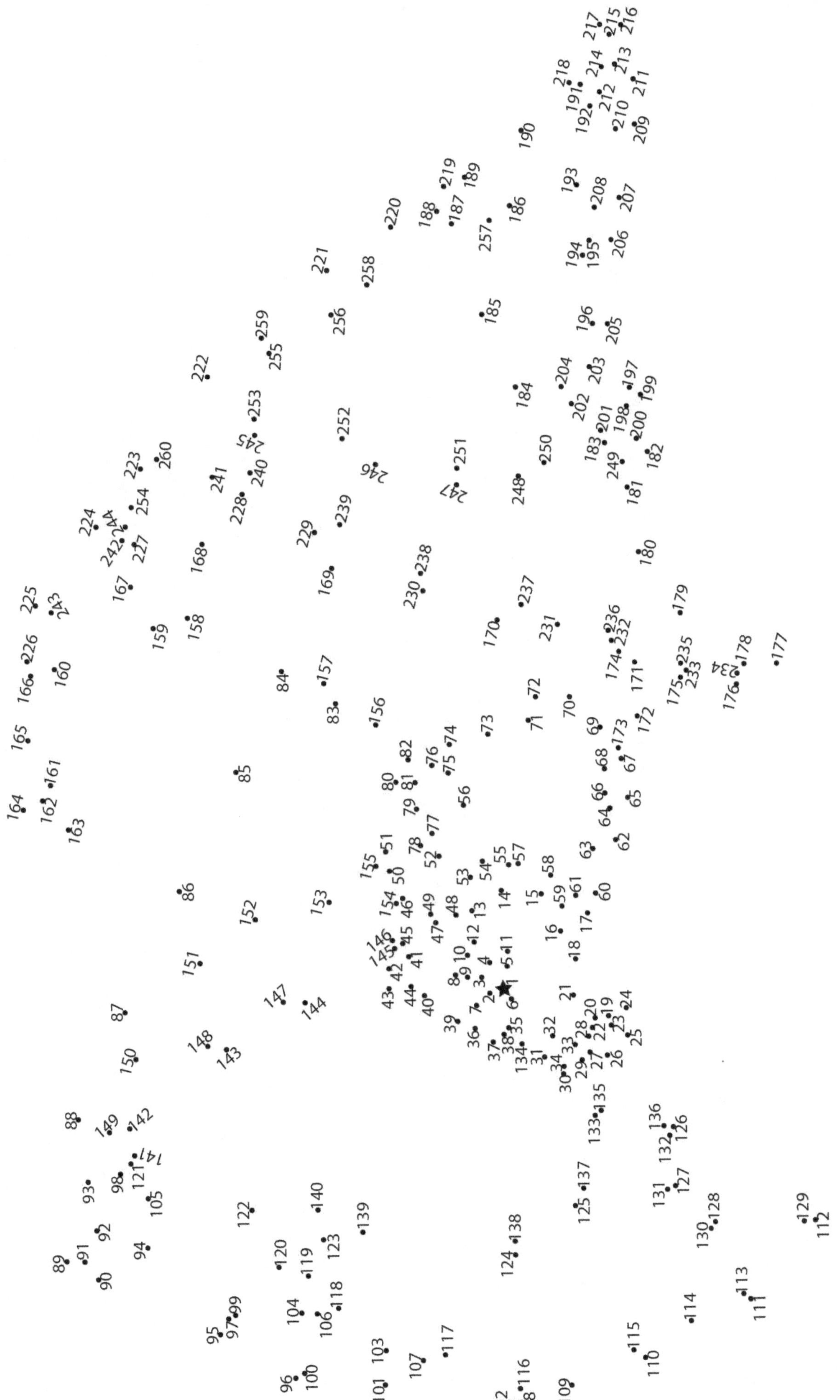

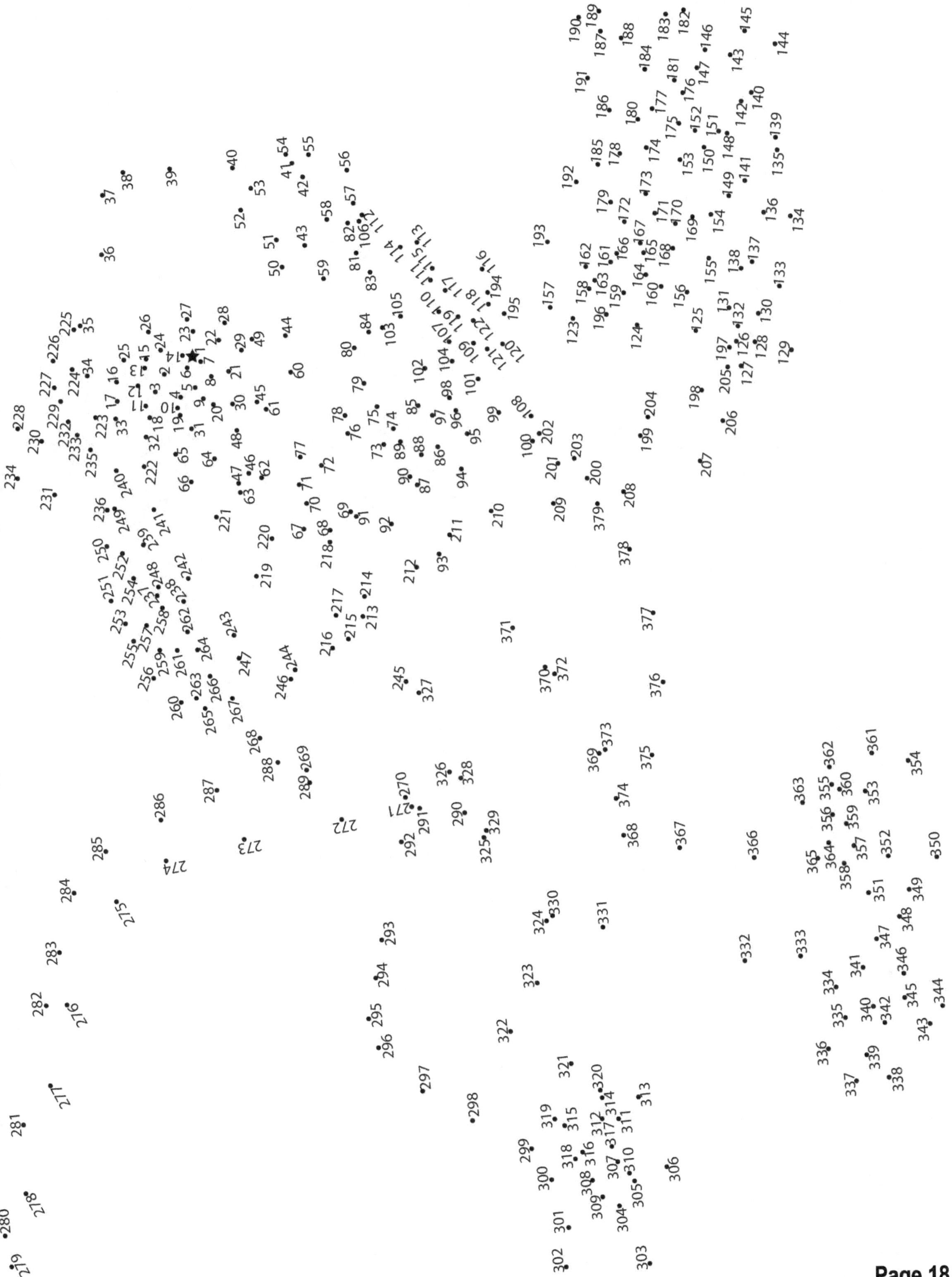

Enjoy bonus images from some of our other fun dot-to-dot books

Find all of our books on Amazon

Cute Baby Animals Dot-to-Dot
Puzzles from 150 to 446 Dots

409 411 408 412
396 398 399 410 400 401 407 413 421
397 397 395 403 402 404 422
390 392 393 394 405 406 416 414 420
388 386 387 42 41 423
385 384 43 40 415 419 429 430
382 389 383 376 417 424
377 54 44 39 38 418 425
375 65 55 53 37 426 428 431
373 66 64 57 56 52 45 439
378 63 58 50 46 47 48 49 35 36 427 432
381 67 51 34 434 438
372 62 59 433 437 441 440
379 374 68 61 33 435
380 366 69 10 32 446
371 70 12 11 9 31 442
367 365 306 72 13 4 3 2 8 30 436 443
370 359 71 5 1 445 447
305 307 73 14 6 15 7
368 364 304 308 310 16 22 24 23 29
360 342 303 309 15 14 21 25 28 20 26 27
369 358 343 344 311 328 326 76 17 18 19 80 111 112
363 361 345 357 329 324 323 77 78 79 81 113 120 444
346 362 353 354 341 301 312 327 325 321 110 114 119 121 122 448
352 355 356 340 302 314 316 318 320 322 82 83 109 115 123
339 300 313 315 317 319 84 118 126
347 351 350 299 334 333 332 330 91 90 108 116 117 124 127
338 335 331 288 287 95 89 88 87 86 85 107 125 128
348 349 337 336 298 296 293 289 92 98 101 102 103 104 105 106 129
143 297 295 294 292 290 286 93 94 96 97 99 100 136 135 134 133 132 131 130
142 144 141 282 140 291 139 138 137 241 240 231 230 221 220 211 210 212
281 145 274 273 283 284 285 250 249 239 229 222 219 209
280 266 265 258 257 242 232 213 208
275 272 264 256 251 248 238 228 223 218 214
146 267 259 252 247 233 227 224 217 207
279 276 271 268 263 260 255 237 234 216 215 206
147 244 226 225 163
148 278 277 270 269 262 261 254 253 246 245 236 235 204 205 172
196 197 198 199 200 201 202 181 203 173 171 164 162
149 195 194 192 193 189 187 188 183 182 180 176 175 174 170 165
150 191 190 184 179 177 167 168 169 160 161
151 186 185 178 159
152 153 154 155 156 157 158

Beautiful Flowers and Butterflies
Dot-to-Dot for Adults

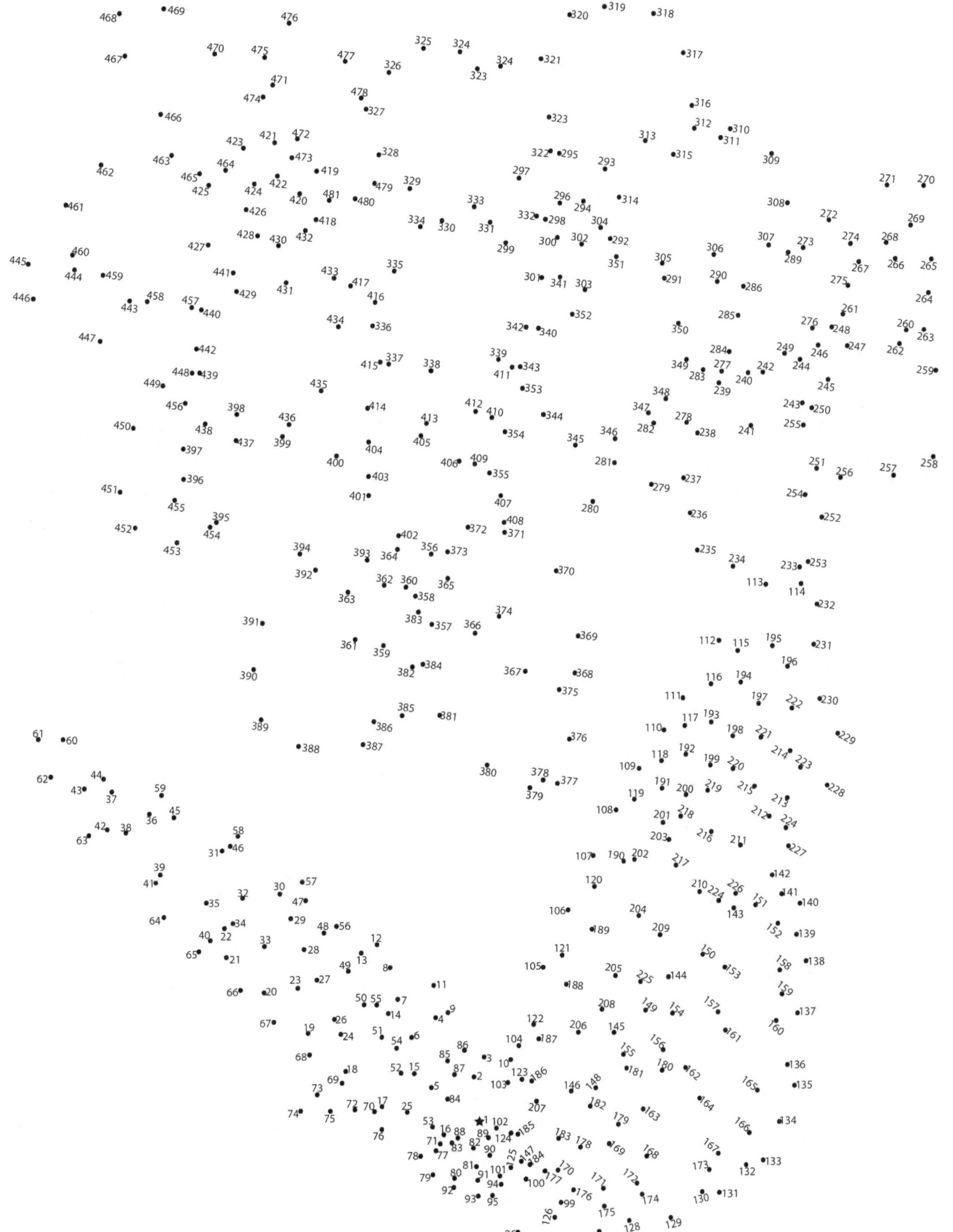

ANSWER KEY

Follow along with the
page numbers from top left
to bottom right

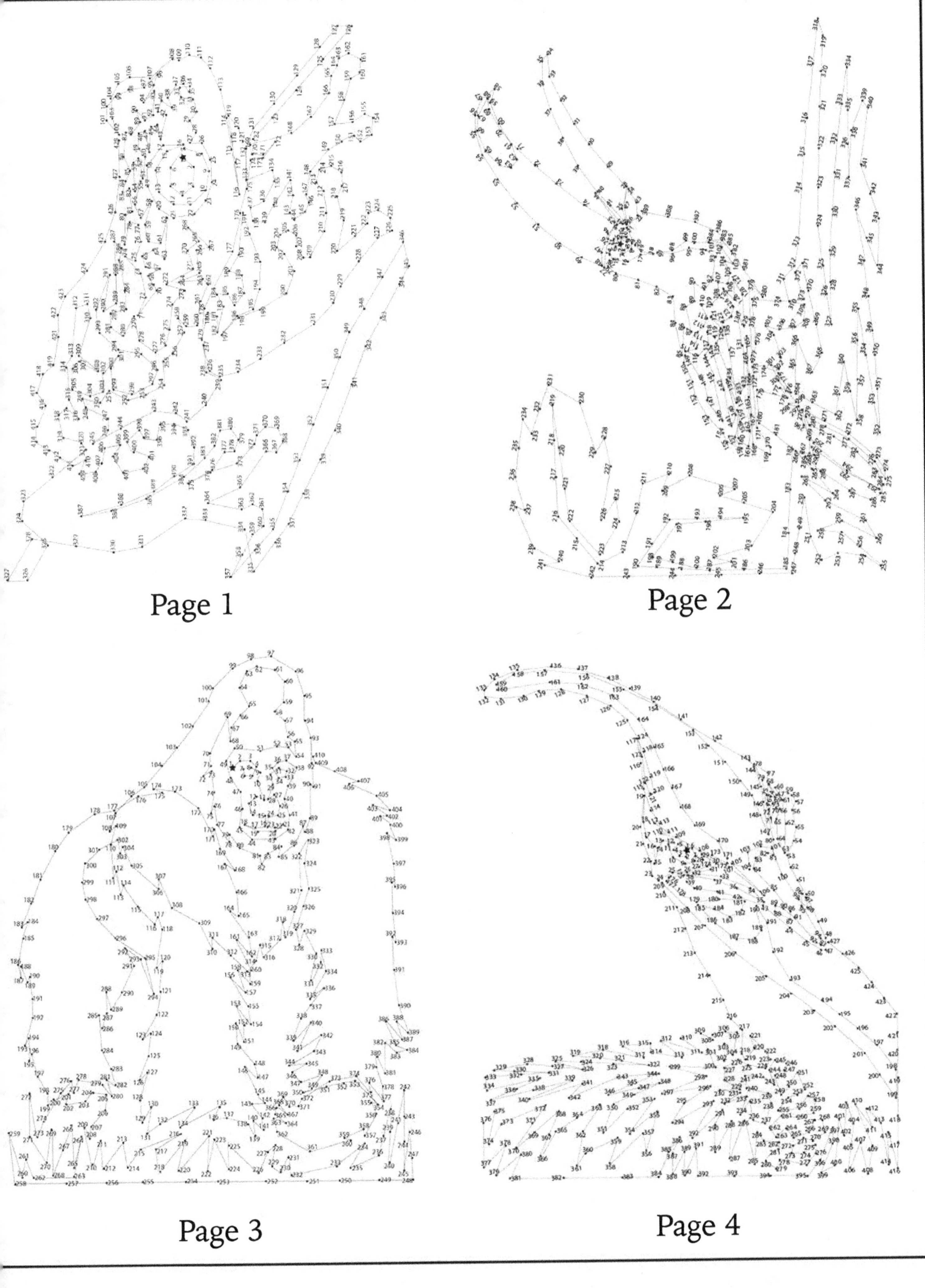

Page 1

Page 2

Page 3

Page 4

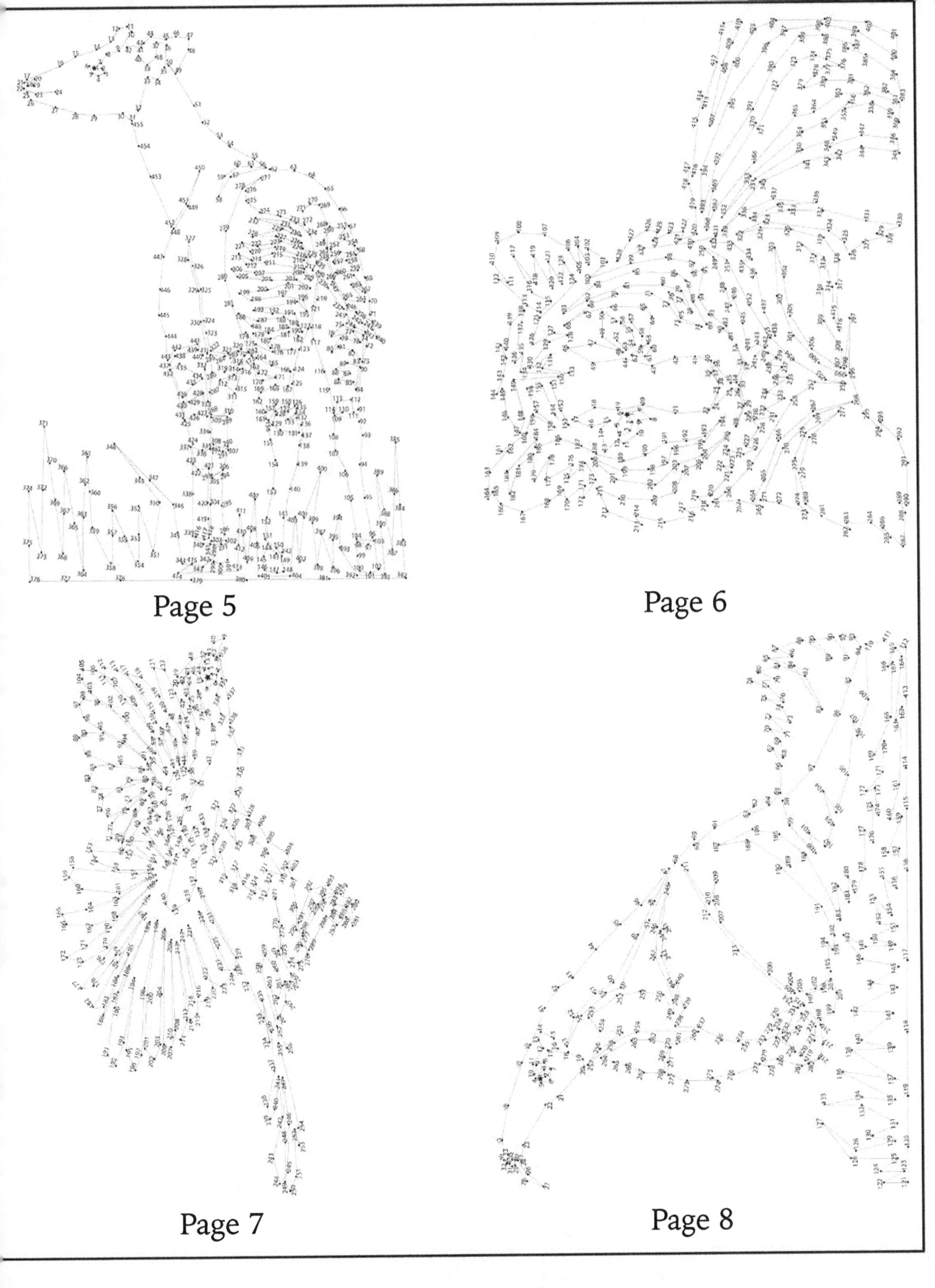

Page 5

Page 6

Page 7

Page 8

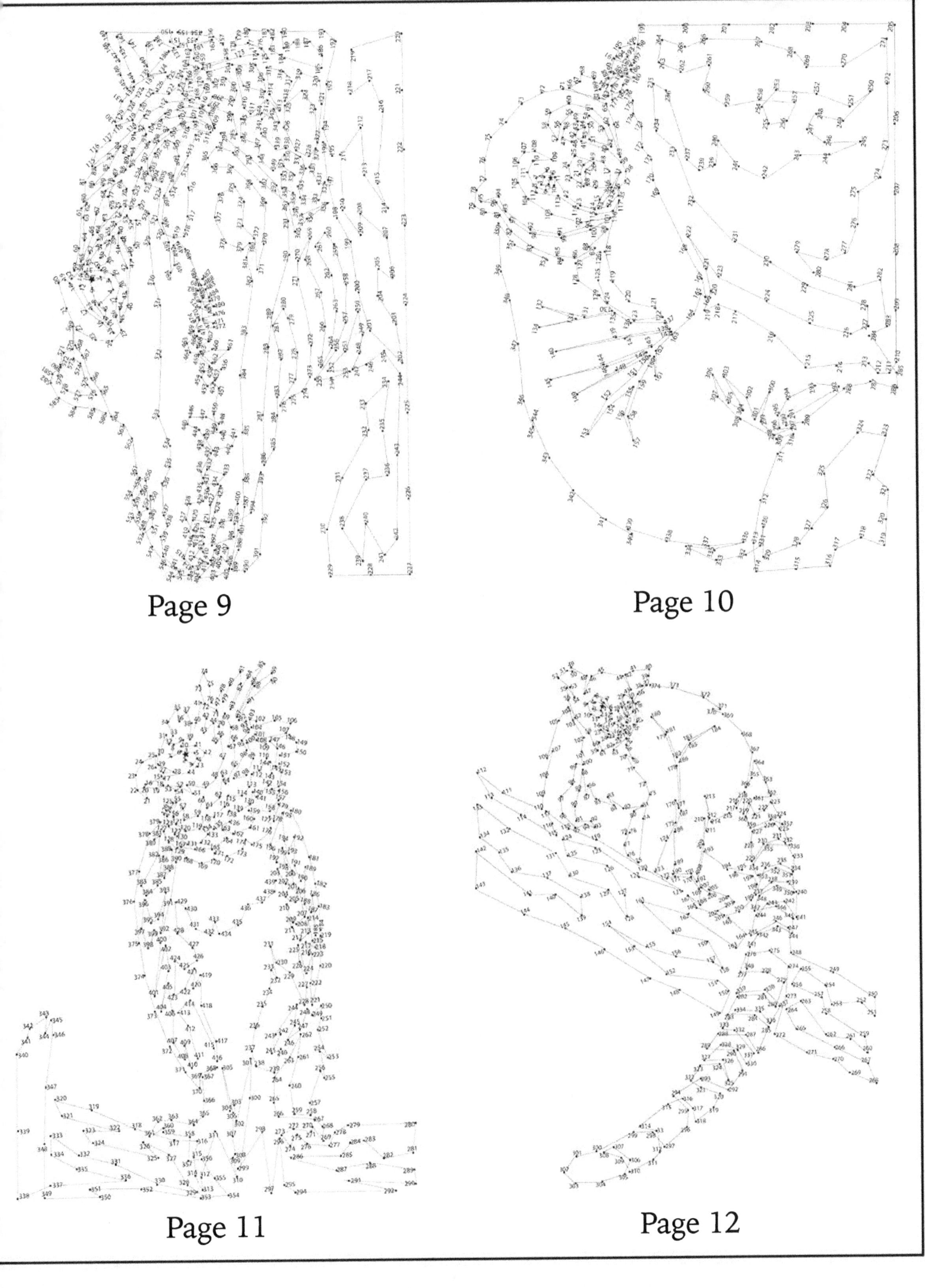

Page 9

Page 10

Page 11

Page 12

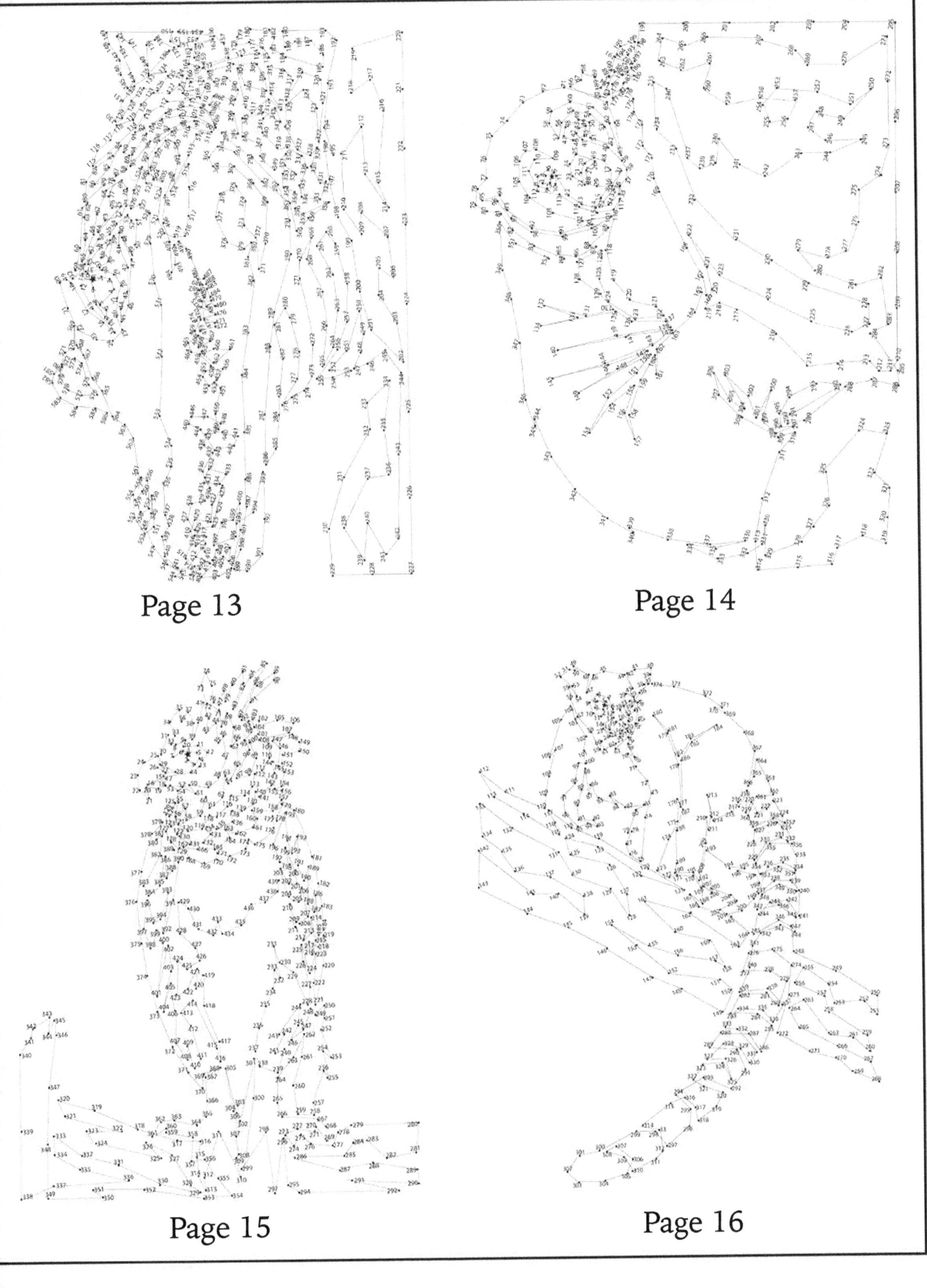

Page 13

Page 14

Page 15

Page 16

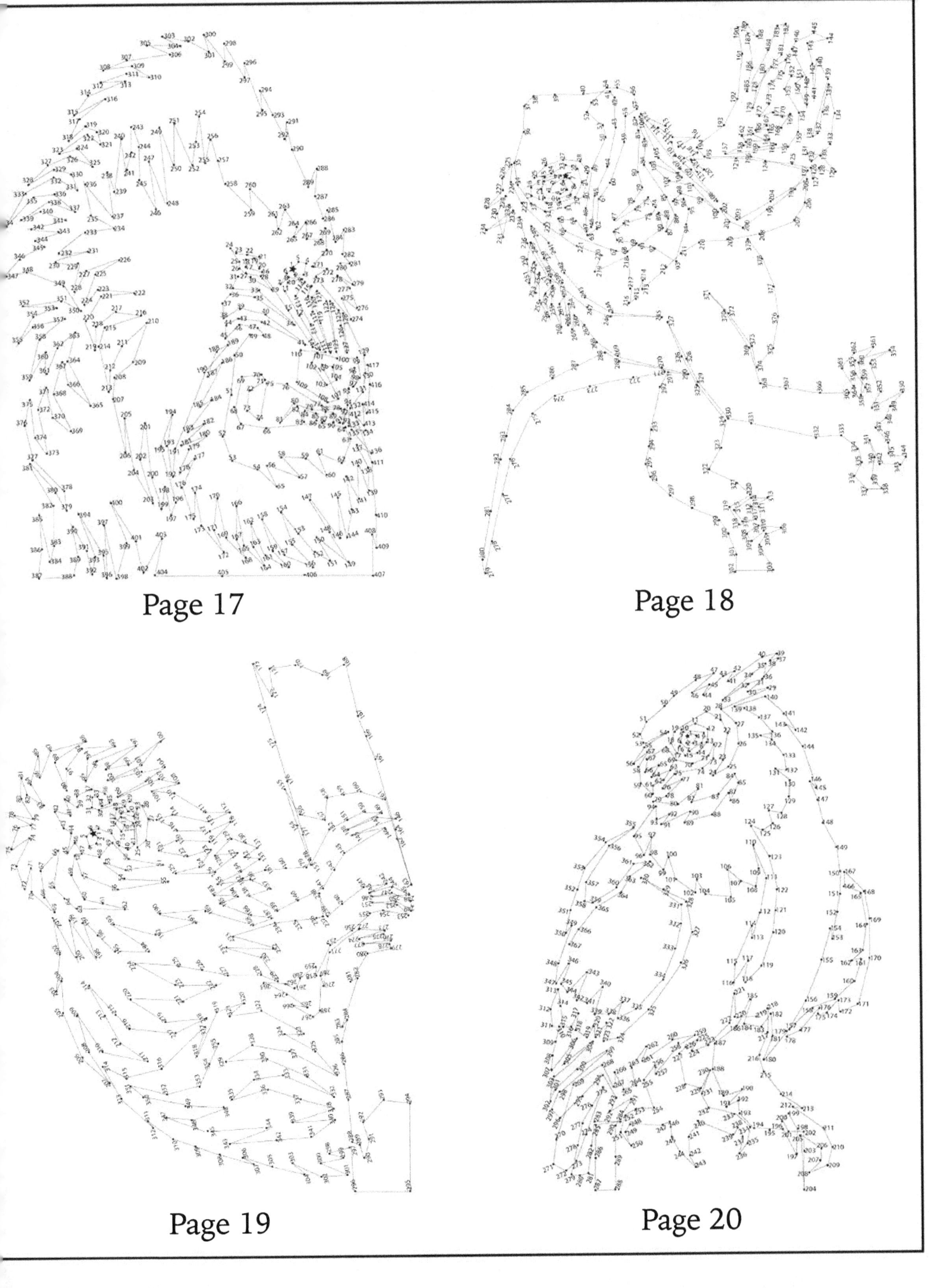

Page 17

Page 18

Page 19

Page 20

Please
Leave
Us
A Review
On Amazon